Watch Me Do Yoga

For Miles and Jake

Library of Congress Cataloging-in-Publication Data
Clennell, Bobby, 1943-
  Watch me do yoga / written and illustrated by Bobby Clennell. — 1st ed.
    p. cm.
  Summary: A young girl practices yoga poses with her father, her mother, and the family dog in the garden, the patio, and her bedroom, always thinking about her connection to the natural world around her.
  ISBN 978-1-930485-26-6 (paper over board : alk. paper)
  [1. Stories in rhyme. 2. Yoga—Fiction.] I. Title.
  PZ8.3.C5577Wat 2010
  [E]—dc22   2010016004

Printed and bound in China
First Edition
ISBN 978-1-930485-26-6
19 18 17 16 15   2 3 4 5 6 7 8

Editors: Linda Cogozzo, Holly Hammond
Cover and Text Design: Gopa & Ted2, Inc.
Author Photographer: Jake Clennell
Lithographer: Union Printing Co.
Text set in Malonia Voigo
Distributed by Publishers Group West

Watch Me Do
YOGA

WRITTEN AND ILLUSTRATED BY BOBBY CLENNELL

RODMELL PRESS

I like to stand upon one leg,

Pretending I'm a tree,

And then I wave my arms about.

Hey, Daddy, look at me!

I practice Mountain Pose with Mom,

We both stand straight and tall,

And then I'll be a swimming fish

With little brother Paul.

My dog and I, we greet the Sun,
And how are you today?

And then we practice Downward Dog,
Before we go and play.

Daddy, let's do Lion Pose,

Stick out our tongues and roar!

Then could you hold me upside down?

Is this what arms are for?

Daddy, Daddy, watch me

Lie down upon the mat,
Then push my hands and feet down
And lift my spine and back.

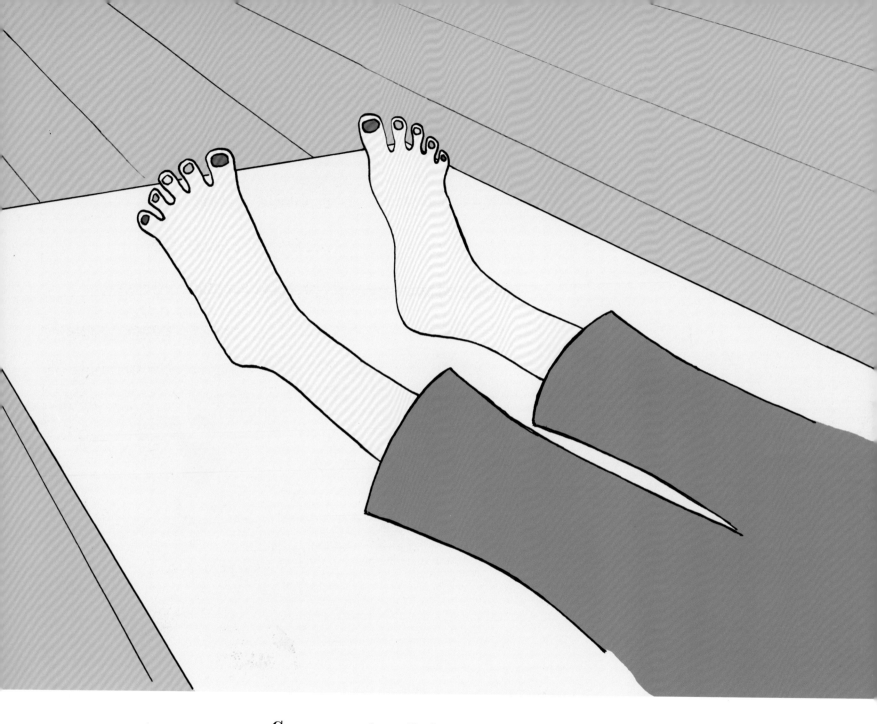

See me sit with legs outstretched.
Can you wiggle your toes like me?

I can sit up straight and strong.
Can you lift your chest? Let's see!

Hey, Mommy, let's do yoga!

See my Tortoise Pose.

I can sleep inside my shell

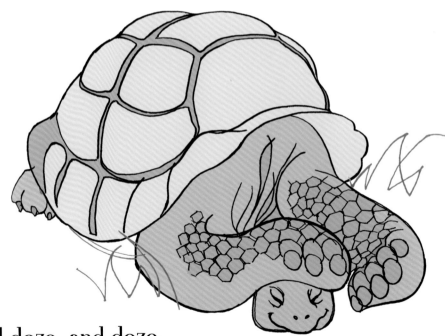

And doze, and doze, and doze.

A lotus flower blossoms
On the surface of the lake.

I fold my legs toward me,
Eyes closed, to meditate.

Child's Pose is easy.
I finish with this pose.
I kneel, then put my head down

So the ground is near my nose.